POETRY IN BLUE

Reflections In The Eye Of A Cop

By

James Patrick McMann

Good Times Publishing
PO Box 4545
Utica, NY 13504

POETRY IN BLUE

Reflections In The Eye Of A Cop

By

James Patrick McMann

Library of Congress Cataloging-in-Publication Data

McMann, James Patrick, 1938-
    Poetry in blue : reflections in the eye of a cop / by James Patrick McMann.
        p.   cm.
        ISBN 0-9639290-3-8
        1. City and town life--New York (N.Y.)--Poetry. 2. Police--New York (N.Y.)--Poetry. 3. Crime--New York (N.Y.)--Poetry. I. Title.
PS3563.C3859P64   1995
811'.54--dc20
                                                                95-41606
                                                                    CIP

Printed in Oneida County, New York

I find poetry a brilliant path to new vistas, one free of thorns or detours. Once I embark on this journey into the mind's eye, I free myself from the chains of fatigue that wrap so tightly around me in the course of my work. We all need escape from the four walls of monotony; for me, writing is the ship to peace.

James Patrick McMann
Utica, NY

3-10-11 Gift

Dedication

Dedicated to every police officer who ever wore a shield in the New York City Police Department.

Acknowledgments

It seems, as I look back upon my life, that I can see a network of friends and loved ones who have helped me and encouraged me in many different, but equally important ways.

I would like to thank:

The three great men who literally saved my life; Donald Reed, Dr. Daricott Vaughn and Dr. Neil Bander.

Friends who provided support and encouragement; Roberta Ellis, Dr. Janice Jackson, Tom Bellini, John Pellicano, Sonny Marianetti, Danny Greene, Billy Leuhrs, Ron Airy, Sgt. Jack Burton, Nancy Kobryn, Joe and Kathy Kelly, Dick Friedrich, Tom Lenahan, Jim and Katie Hagan, Elizabeth Szlek

My wonderful children Maryrose, Daniel and Lindabeth for their unending love. I thank them, too, for my three precious grandchildren, Stephanie, Eddie and tiny Kaitlyn Rose.

Thank you all for blessing my life.

Foreword

Jimmy McMann dreamt about the Major Leagues. At sixteen, his knuckle ball attracted the attention of baseball scouts, and as the star pitcher, he lead his high school team to a winning season. But for Jimmy, the Big Leagues were to come in another form: He became one of New York's Finest, a Police Officer in the New York City Police Department.

After serving as a Marine in such exotic locales as Crete, Naples, Beirut and Turkey, he returned to Utica, New York, and joined the Utica Police Department. Still, dreams of the "Majors" never left him, and after nine years on the force he took the test for the New York Police Department. He was summoned to the Police Academy in 1973.

As a strange combination of rookie/veteran, Jimmy received his first assignment: The notorious 42nd Precinct of the South Bronx, next to "Fort Apache", where he was to spend seven years engaged in guerrilla warfare with a population high in pushers, pimps and arsonists. This was life on the wild side, and the police fortified themselves with demon rum to meet the horrors of each tour.

It was in the Bronx that Jimmy began to write. His short story, "Welcome to the South Bronx" detailed a single night's adventure in this urban wilderness, and it won a prize from a local writer's society. Jimmy was hooked. He'd found a way to translate the chaos around him into order by capturing it on paper. He recalled the poetry of Poe which so mesmerized him as a young boy, the etchings of Dante's Inferno by Dore, the works of Milton in Paradise Lost. He became enamored of the music of Richard Wagner, its complex harmonies providing a kind of microcosm of the troubled, swirling city around him. Raw evil, power, brutal clashes with gruesome forces of malice, and senseless violence were his daily companions. He took this stuff and made it into art.

New York has over 32,000 Police Officers. All of them face danger and death each day. When they assemble to turn out, no one knows if the friend beside him will survive that tour of duty. They respond to this pressure in 32,000 different ways. Some devote themselves to an acting career, some write novels, some become lawyers, some raise horses. One man dreams of raising yew trees to provide an anti-cancer drug, Taxol; another drives to his little house on the edge of the battlefield in Gettysburg and spends his weekends painstakingly recreating the entire battle on a 215 foot square table in his basement. Many, unfortunately, turn to drink and some to drugs, to numb themselves.

Jimmy McMann found his poetic voice to help him cope with the unending drama of New York life. He defines the job police officers do as "humans protecting humans from humans". Alas, nothing human is foreign to him, and from his cynosure at the center of the universe, Times Square, he has seen it all.

Jimmy's dream of the Big Leagues ended on September 21, 1988, when he was attacked by a mentally disordered man - a Cuban refugee from the Mariel boat lift - who came within a millimeter of killing him. "Murder in Saint Patrick's Cathedral" - a bigger-than-life headline, brought an end to his cherished career as one of New York's Finest. But it did little to dampen his charm and wit, his desire to tell his stories and read his poems to all who would listen. Jimmy loves many things: As "Jimmy Banks" he is a tournament-winning pool player; as a fanatic Wagnerite he tells of riding to a police emergency to the booming strains of the "Ride of the Valkyries"; as an aficionado of old films and radio, you will find him glued to the AMC channel watching "Detective Story"; or, you may find him proclaiming in wonderment when the Pleiades appear on a starry Adirondack night. But what Jimmy loves most is the New York City Police. This book is for them.

Elizabeth Szlek
Utica, NY

Poetry in Blue

*All cops dread this
announcement over their
radios, "West 50th Street,
D.O.A." This was written
just after the Morgue
Wagon's departure.*
1980

James P. McMann

DOA

I remember a naked fat man one night
Dead for a week in his cluttered room
With roaches and maggots on his face
The stench of Hell around him loomed

Breaking the windows that were nailed shut
Night air attacking the putrid stink
I observed the room in which he died
A soiled bed, a broken chair, a filthy sink

Newspapers piled high in yellowed form
Headlines now dead, dead as he
Long forgotten stories of joy and peace
Stories of hope he never did see

He was just a line in a cop's memo book
Without family or friends to simply say
How much they dearly loved this man
Or to retrieve his body on his death day

The morgue wagon with its heartless crew
Arrived and how his fat body sagged
Under their straining and cursing task
Forcing his rotting girth in a rubber bag

Then yelling and swearing down the stairs
Tossing him headlong into their van
Crashing on other bags collected this night
Then off to the morgue with the forgotten man.

On West 46th Street near 9th Ave we had to remove junkies from a "shooting gallery". While searching the tenement I found a young woman on the roof. I wrote this after speaking to her .
1979

CURIOSITY

Upon a rooftop I asked a girl one day
Just a cop and an addict in brilliant May
"What made you start down this road?"
"Curiosity," came the voice, lost, cold.

Then out poured her dreadful tale
Of innocence destroyed, a life failed
Bright child once, sheltered against fear
So long ago, yesterday, a thousand years

She showed withered, collapsed veins
Tunnels of life poisoned by injected pain
I looked into eyes of an old young woman
Seeking death on the installment plan

Skin popping stings at first
Just a pinch to satisfy a thirst
Mainlining, sweet, destroying harm
Flowing bright dream into an arm

Snort that "H" into a nose
Excited sniffing, freedom flows
Illusionary escape, powdered white
Frozen demon face, smiling fright

Taken for possession, a slave's crime
She floated through court without time
Back to needles dripping with doom
Before reaching twenty-three...her tomb.

*I was in the hotel
room where the master
playwright was found dead.
While I waited around with
other cops, I wrote this
poem about his life.
1981*

WILLIAMS' STREET CAR

Desire lives not in graveyards
It ends with the last gasping breath
Like a flaming torch in hot life
That fades then vanishes in cold death

Loneliness is a grave each day
Dark is its coffin in reality's sight
Terrifying are the ice fingers that touch the heart
Trapped in a sunken tomb away from light

Humans who thirst for compassion's hand
Will seek out strangers for a brief moment
Losing themselves in pretending arms
Then returning to the grave when the encounter is spent

Blanche DuBois was his altered self
Frightened, drowning soul in a sea of hate
Belittled by cruelty's merciless voice
Buried in illusions that sealed their fate.

Written aboard the "D" train to the Bronx. It reminded me of birth and death. Sliding doors for arriving and departure .
1986

SUBWAY

Train of life racing through days
Crowded with strangers on their way
Unknown sources to unknown places
Travelers in time, all creeds, all races

Destiny is the tunnel in which it roars
At each stop, through its sliding doors
The old, all spent, slowly reluctantly leave
The young race on, eager dreams to weave

Destinations in windows flash on by
Only the poet, observing, says why
Middle-aged faces like mannequins staring
Not at death or birth, just frozen, uncaring

Terrified of this life's recording book
Fear of seeing their name if they look
So they ride on in selfishness' name
At their lonely stop, they leave, themselves to blame

This subway speeds on tracks called years
Alive with valiant hopes, dead with coward's fears
A one way trip for you and me
Streaming ever on into eternity.

The Midtown North Precinct was a madhouse parade of human suffering one August night. T o escape, I went up onto the station house roof and beheld the full moon and wrote the following.
1989

EVENING

When all souls seek desired rest
I gaze upon my silver ship, conquest
It glides, silent, in sea of satin blue
Distant suns, gleaming like cities, breaking through

Will it stream onward towards their shores?
If only I could sail in its mystical core
Brilliant brightness, what treasures to find
Vessel of dreamers, lamp of my mind

Hail, evening! Soothing maiden of peace
Never your calming perfume cease
May your glowing ship greet eternity
Carrying my heart, safe, joyous, free.

One learns humility quickly in this house of death. This poem was jotted down in my memo book as a way to escape the stress and terror cops see in all the morgues across the land.

1982

James P. McMann

MANHATTAN MORGUE

Sliding slabs that swallow all up
Holding the remains of New York life
Naked except for a tag on their toes
Most dead through mayhem and strife

One four-hundred-pounder died while choking
Like a beached whale in human flesh
A chicken wing was found gorged in his throat
Temperature a little lower to keep him fresh

Another slab holds a young beauty
Just twenty, when her wrists were slit
Deserted by her lover, she chose her way
Leaving this world in a despairing fit

Along side a window washer, his belt broke
The terror look still in his open eyes
Fell from seventeen stories this day
His twisted mouth uttering no cries.

An old man of ninety is crumpled here
His face purple from the suicide rope
What a crime for a human so close
To the door of salvation, then lose all hope

So the slabs fill up around the clock
In this roaring city that never sleeps
Cold are the attendants at their task
Only the observer pauses to weep.

While observing a reddish moon over the Hudson River, I wrote this in a radio car in a moment of desired escape through reverie ... 54th and Twelfth Avenue.

1985

James P. McMann

SEPTEMBER MOON

A murder world hangs on high
Blood color is its ancient dust
Rivers of crimson swiftly falling
Over mountains of gleaming rust

Lantern of silver no longer streams
Whiteness drowned by pulsating red
Leaving the gazer to only see
Soaking plasma of a billion dead

Blaze on, orb of scarlet glow
Beautiful auburn on your secrets past
Painting your oceans and valleys deep
A spell over dreamers you have cast

When slumber covers my lifeless form
I'll drift above your molten face
Descending to silence of sleeping death
Sinking into liquid of a slaughtered race.

I wrote this aboard the Metro North commuter train along the Hudson River. The fog shimmered in a crevice of t h e Palisades and it called my name.
1985

FOG

Clouds hung low on my river today
Like Indian smoke signals drifting
Upward amid the rocky cliffs circling
White funnels, like fingers - lifting

Twilight in daytime, gray face crying
Mist-breath calling softly to me
"Drink in my dream brew, observing man
And my secrets you will surely see"

"Find rapture in my cleansing vapors
Bathe your face in my purifying sprays
For within my intoxicating liquid potion
You will be rejuvenated your remaining days"

So I stood in the fog-draped shafts rising
Feeling the soothing wet being invading mine
Washing fears away ever gently
Embraced by a transparent wonder, so gloriously fine.

After I heard Greta Garbo had died alone in her uptown apartment, I thought of her final moments.
1990

James P. McMann

GARBO

Silver screen of yesterday fading
Death is at her door waiting
While she sits in her chamber dark
Wrinkled body, unkempt, stark

Past lovers rot within their tombs
Whispering specters around her swoon
Bathing an old ego with compliments
Voices denying her life is spent

Gnarled fingers start the machine
She is young again in the silver beam
In a sea tale, salty and misty
Youth reborn as "Anna Christie"

The scenes grind on as she slumps in her chair
In this brief life, she has ceased to care
While on the screen, lovely features, graceful tones
And in the dark, from cold lips, "alone".

My post on Times Square had video machine galleries where young boys sold themselves to men. Written in the Midtown North Precinct after arrest. 1984

BOY WITH THE
COAL BLACK HAIR

I first spotted him running on Broadway
Being desired by leering, tortured men
Through arcades of whirling machines
Pedophiles seeking this boy of ten

Not seeing me, they came down the street
Hand in hand, yet not father and son
Wide-eyed tourists never knowing
Child-loving adult and the prize he'd won

I studied their trip to the nearest hotel
With security guard I went to their room
Unlocking the door, an unnatural sight
Naked hell around them loomed

A camera on a dresser taped
Recording the lust for future eyes
Oddities locked together burning
In fire created by the Father of Lies

Dressing with curses, arrest was made
Both to the station house were brought
Two lost souls standing in the light
Seducer and the child he'd bought

Back to his mother went the kid
In a week he returned to Times Square
Male prostitute, destroyed and dying,
Only ten, the boy with the coal black hair.

Cold vision the Hudson River in t h e bitterest of months frozen m o m e n t s, f r o z e n memories.
1984

James P. McMann

FEBRUARY ALONG
THE HUDSON

February's silver mournful face
Gray light beams from misty eyes
River like listless tears of woe
It is the month of despairing sighs

The earth between the water edges
Is fog draped, floating fingers of doom
Coating the landscape in garments of the grave
Like a chilling, silent twilight tomb

It is Winter Death's last frigid breath
Being overwhelmed by the approaching light
That will burn away all ice-heart dreams
A phoenix rising of flowers, gloriously bright

Then once the miracles have returned to man
He will remember the month that lonely weeps
Wondering on what melancholy journey it has gone
Forgetting it is here, waiting, sorrow filled, asleep.

*Purple   d e a t h
banners across a station
house   e n t r a n c e
announced to all that a
police officer had been
killed in the line of duty. In
the dreadful South Bronx,
the banners seemed to be
always rippling.
1974*

James P. McMann

42nd PRECINCT

Warrior garrison at Washington and Third
Around it the drums of poverty are heard
Welcome to the South Bronx of 'Seventy-three
Steel your nerves for what you'll see

Hot is the heroin in summer's heat
Anxiously injected into arms, legs, feet
Block upon block of roach-filled rooms
Tormentors of the poor in misery tombs

Fires are set by arson hordes
Hired by avaricious landlords
Burn them with flame, kill them with smoke
The furnace of human greed to stoke

Under the el, the fortress stands
Blue is the color of its soldier bands
In the darkness of crime, a lighted tower
Circling beacon in evil's blackest hour

Day into night terror never stops
Murdered strangers, assassinated cops
Purple death crepe above its door
Casualties rising, American war.

·

After hearing a self
-centered captain rant after
missing out on promotion
test.   Memo   book
reflections.
1984

EGO

Oh, fragile inner little self
You so need praise-flowered wine
Intoxicant flowing lifts heart high
What addiction this eternal voice of mine

As if made of delicate porcelain
That insult or sarcasm can cruelly dash
Causing eruptions of anguish raging
How the heart is mercilessly lashed

Yet it rises anew through gratification
That narcotic, compliment, lifts from its tomb
It lives again through momentary glory
When ego controls, the egotist is doomed.

Written after I worked the opening of O'Neill's classic vision of family destruction, remembering my own Irish family's despair.

1987

James P. McMann

"LONG DAY'S JOURNEY", REREAD

O'Neill's family rising from their tombs
Ghosts of unhappiness upon the stage
Painful terror flowed from his pen
People united by blood inflaming rage

Celtic tapestry, this miserable clan
Dark moods swirling, these Irish minds
Alcohol is a river of the lost
Sink into its depths in order to find

A world of cynicism, laden with chains
At the bottom of a harbor, the past
Currents of recrimination drifting by
Within the eyes of the viewers are cast

Tidal waves of truth from acted words
Fog clouds smothering, fog horn calling
Family, oh family, sepulcher so cold
Death wings, as night comes falling.

Written as a reflection in a mirror, a bitter reminder of loss and a renewed hope o f forgiveness.
1970

James P. McMann

SONG OF
DIVORCED DADS

Children, children of my heart
Where does a divorced father start?
Children, children growing up without me
No greater sorrow for a man can there be

Days into weeks, weeks into long years
Lonely rooms, memories, hot longing tears
My calling memory won't let me forget
And I have to clash each morn with regret

How do I start my life again
When all I think about is way back then?
Children, children, please forgive me
Look into my grieving heart and maybe you'll see

A lost father who needs his daughters and fine lads
To take him and kiss him, saying, "We forgive you, Dad."
And after receiving that God given wealth
He can start again by forgiving himself.

This poem is dedicated to:

> Maryrose
> Michael
> Daniel
> Lindabeth

Note: This poem was published by Ann Landers in her daily column at the time it was written.

A tortured couple who lived on West 55th Street. We made countless runs to separate their self-hating battles. An observation of marriage.
1979

James P. McMann

UNITED STRANGERS

Her cold eyes gazed at his heartless face
Through each cold room silence went
Though wedded for the last twenty years
They'd forgotten what to each other they had meant

Separate tables, separate strangers in a cafe
Not caring, never knowing, each with its own tale
When the sleeping chamber is separated by two
Warning sounds for the relationship to fail

Although they prance together for all to see
Seemingly happy when acting for family and friends
They smile and laugh for the observer's sake
But between two bleeding hearts, different messages
        they send

Like zombies they leave the approving crowd
Sinking into loathing when again all alone
Just blind human beings not seeking a way out
Content only to exist, with internal cries, moans

That in the end will destroy even their lives
By crushing them ever closer to the heart of regret
For not letting each be free to find a glorious shore
Where at last their day of mutual cruelty can set

On any street, in any town across the land
They live united in pretense only
Dead in feelings, dead in desire, hopeless
Strangers living in the soul of the lonely.

Clouded inner thoughts of redemption, pondered while walking along railway tracks at night.
1986

James P. McMann

NIGHT TRAIN

Walking under the shimmering moon one night
I came upon two steel rails glistening in the light
Then I heard the moaning eerie cry
Like a banshee, across the liquid sky

Its mournful voice called out to me
"Dark-drenched traveler, hear my sighs and you see
Within this sound lies the secret of all man's sorrow
Discover it, and you will find joy on the new morrow"

I listened within my happiness seeking mind
Desperately hoping in each echoing wail to find
The elixir that would cleanse my heart
Erasing all despair, for a new start

But alas, it was only hopelessness that led me to believe
And the haunting, lonely calling my soul did weave
A mystical yearning that could never really be
Leaving only reality in its chilling, fading plea.

*Living in the world
of today, yet thinking of
long ago.*
1988

BYPASSED ROAD

A once-used road buried in grass
Forgotten by today's modern means
An overgrown concrete pathway
Traveled only in yesterday's dreams

I stood and looked deeply at its course
Oh, how I lovingly remembered and stared
Seeing gleaming people-packed vehicles
From a more peaceful era when we cared

Then suddenly, I was in a '48 Buick
Silently cruising over this newly built road
Passing houses of another time
With little stands where Orange Crush was sold

A taste of nectar no longer made
A glassful of sweetness for just pennies
And from the house's lace-curtained window
the clean laughter created by Jack Benny

Brought back to reality by impatient shouts
I leave the weeds covering all traces
Of people who traveled seeking life
In American cars to safe and clean places

I have thought of the highway going nowhere
Wanting to find it and longingly see
Sitting along side it in darkness, watching
For a '48 Buick, its headlights glowing brightly.

Poetry in Blue

While on my post in a horrific rainstorm, I took refuge in the Howard Johnson's Restaurant at West 46th Street and Broadway. Over hot tea I wrote this.

1987

James P. McMann

THUNDER AND LIGHTNING

Mountains of black smoke rolling
Into each other in a colossal clash
Of forces so potent
His knowledge comes with the lightning flash

Exploding from the billowing turbulent war
A jagged finger of burning light
An arrow from electricity's heart
Ripping with unimagined might

Turning ebony into blazing day
Piercing the forest with streaks of fire
Consuming majestic aged trees
Destroying their grace on a roaring pyre

When clouds of heat come into cold
Rival battle lines quickly form
Two armies beyond our nightmare dreams
Who fight to the death in thunder storms.

> *A clock repair shop*
> *on Ninth Ave had a huge*
> *clock in its window whose*
> *hands sped around rapidly.*
> *I wrote this poem after*
> *dreaming of that shop.*
> *1986*

DREAM ON TIME

Purple midnight, blaze of youth
Came glowing down my street
Streak of light passed on by
Hair aflame, with wings on feet

"My name is Time, I cannot stop,"
I heard him whisper from the fire
"Controlling men my earthly task,
Into tomorrow - I never tire"

Beside this arrow, amazed I watched
Melting horizons, Time and me
Frantic his cry, "The void is near!
There it swirls, boundless Eternity!"

Before my eyes a whirlpool churned
Circling silence, a terror yawned
White explosion dissolved the lad
Star shine, waking, shimmering dawn.

Manhattan was wrapped in thick fog one night and thoughts of this wondrous creation were placed on paper.
1985

James P. McMann

FOG DREAM

Colossal sheets descending
Covering air in liquid gray
Smothering clouds upon the earth
Silent intruder to this day

Fingers winding round my throat
Cutting off precious sweet breath
All visions fading into ghosts
Figure approaching, smiling Death

Lifting my corpse in swirling mist
Wrapping this form in gleaming cloak
Upwards to its twilight world
Eternity of blindness in shapeless smoke.

*Leaving the city
after a 6 PM - 2 AM tour.
Metro North commuter train
- moonlight reflecting.
1985*

TRAIN WINDOW

Flashing by the window near me
Speeding visions my eyes do see
Like a moving film of pastoral scenes
A fleeting reflection of created dreams

River shimmering like diamonds, out my pane
Emerald forests covering darkened lanes
Where secrets lie unseen by man
Written in dust by specter hands

Boulders are seen, then are gone
For that brief moment they sing their song
Of saints and fools they've seen rise and fall
Hearing their prayers and defiant calls

Down through the ages when glaciers ruled
Grinding and crushing, gleaming like jewels
Polished smooth by collisions vast
Beyond my streaking life they will last

Graveyards swoosh by in blinding blur
Movers and shakers of yesterday, him and her
Just a glimpse of their final slumber this day
Flashing tombstones into the future mark my way

Destination! I slowly depart
Leaving in my window a poet's heart
Dissolving into my sanctuary with a sigh
Marveling at treasures that in contemplation lie.

On vacation in Pennsylvania, written while sitting near the North Carolina monument.
1986

James P. McMann

GETTYSBURG

Call to arms, clashing shields
Marching men across a field
Load the breech with steel chains
Shot of death to kill and maim

Stars flutter above the gray
American blood splashed this day
Through boys bullets mortally tore
Prideful price for a civil war

Row upon row of southern youth
Slaughtered for ideas they thought truth
A lad of eighteen, so young to die
Slumped with his rifle, in Brady's eye

Bloated bodies by a farmer's hedge still
Rotting remains of courage pledged
Captured on film for all to see
Fallen brothers in the land of the free

Their stones still gleaming over the years
Also dead, the weeping tears
Monuments in granite, chiseled deep
Grace the sanctuary in which they sleep.

Deserted factory
crumbling in the Bronx.
Written while on patrol in the
42nd precinct.
1974

James P. McMann

VISIT TO YESTERDAY

Forlorn is the crumbling factory shell
Where once proud workers wove their skill
Making products for America's might
In machine shops, factories and mills

I stand and gaze into deserted rooms
Seeing ghosts of laborers from another age
Hearing their sighs for a time that is past
Reading their names on yesterday's page

Silence in dust is everywhere
Cobwebs of time knotted like rope
Strangling the pride that glowed there
Smothering once bright dreams and hopes

Within these walls I leave a prayer
Remembering a much nobler time back then
Bright faces smiling, fading
I call on God's mercy for those working men.

While I walked up and down the hills of a centuries-old cemetery, the sleepers became pictures in my mind.

1988

FOREST HILL

Up each road past the graves
Faded names in greenish mold
Row on row of slumbering dead
Epitaphs chiseled, wisdom told

A boy of ten lies sleeping there
Lift the veil so I can see
Little James in blissful peace
Brilliant crystal for eternity

Monuments in granite of forgotten wealth
At death they were old or in their youth
Desire and greed not in this ground
A flame forever burns --- truth

Saints and sinner, only God the judge
Sunrise to sunset new plots to fill
One mortal walking as they rest
A passing shadow in Forest Hill.

*This was written at
four o'clock in the morning,
the "darkest hour of night".
Yet, a brilliant moon bathed
me in a peace and I thought
of her lost children.
1989*

James P. McMann

LOST CHILDREN
OF THE MOON

Moonbeams have softly filtered down
Descending over silent hills at night
Giving courage to those who are lost
By dissolving the dark in silver-fingered light

When skies of pitch are blinding all
And the mystery beams are buried deep
Leaving the hills eerie with scary shapes
Bringing the lost only the ability to weep

You heard that wailing across the land
Carried in the hands of ebony to your door
You failed to venture out without God's lamp
Because facing the unknown brought terror to your core

Dawn sounded trumpets for the brave to march by
Fanfares allowing you to look where no man had seen
A million arrows glowing like phosphorous
Those lovely little wayward moonbeams.

After a frightful night of police duty, I was unable to sleep. After writing this, I drifted off into contentment.
1987

SLEEP

Gliding, silent river of darkest realm
Gently carrying slumberers upon its crests
Passing gilded palaces or forests dark
On its journey into heart of rest

It may flow by vistas where no living are
Reflecting departed loved ones shining bright
Who call out our names in glowing tones
Refiring our souls with hope's pure light

The river of ebony upon which we glide
Can plunge without warning into an abyss
Cascading down through nightmare scenes
Horrifying the slumberer with terror's kiss

But fear is only illusion within these currents
And a moment can seem so frightfully long
Screaming in quicksand's grip or with walls closing in
Then, all will vanish in reality's awakening song

For some, however, the river never ceases
Sinking the traveler into fathomless deep
Where peaceful serenity closes the eyes
Being touched by Death, the brother of sleep.

I was inspired by a photograph of a n abandoned lighthouse taken by a friend in New York. The white whale's pursuit and revenge came before me.
1990

LIGHTHOUSE DARK

Swirling beam in grave so dark
Abandoned lighthouse silent, stark
Eye now blind to surging sea
What memories do you sigh to me?

Ships of wood with billowing sails
Tattooed crews who slaughtered whales
Vessels filled with green splashed jade
Which oriental hands so patiently made

Tempest might, crashing waves
All hearts seek a ray to save
Their souls from the boiling foam
But into King Neptune's realm they roam

All sinking far from circling light
Whirlpool of cries in dreadful fright
This was once in the cold dead beam
Shimmering yesterdays, my Melville dream.

*After visiting some
friends in a cemetery, I sat in
my car for a long time.
1989*

James P. McMann

SNOW AND STONES

White sea still with frozen waves
Cold death above and below in graves
Peaceful are the wise, tortured the knaves
Across each stone a bitter wind raves

Winter's oceans of crushing dark
Create an alien landscape, barren, stark
Smooth alabaster, no footfalls mark
Creaking iron sign, "Eternity's Park"

The buried are left beneath the sea
Some are captured, some are free
Cries of sadness, songs of glee
Graveyard truths revealed to me.

Loneliness for all of us is a frightful world. Some escape, while others remain. Written after I stayed too long in a forest. 1986

James P. McMann

STAR SET

Star setting beyond the hill
Glorious lights streaming like fingers
Mesmerized by the fading grace
Melting into darkness, we still linger

Within the web of darkness
We seek one last ember of light
For in finding its shrinking brilliance
We ward off - momentarily - the oncoming night

Now the chill kiss of ebony's visitor is upon us
And we grope our frightful sightless way
Without the moon's silver lamp to guide us
With eyes like morning glories, waiting for the day.

While in the theater detail, "Electra" was playing on Broadway. I wrote this as a reflection of O'Neill's work in my own life.

1985

James P. McMann

MOURNING BECOMES JIMMY

Nail all my windows shut
Smother each of my inner sighs
Bolt the doors, imprison me
For I must live within my lives.

Oh, darkened chamber, hide me here
Alone with dead ancestors swirling
Suicides and God-fearers dance
From their grinning mouths hurling

Coward's lies, truth from the brave
Coaxing me to follow their lead
I curse all tongues that taunt
"Silence!" - I screaming plead.

Electra comes as a silver mist
Covers my eyes with Irish hands
Sleep so gently, soothing falls
The dead, empty house, barren land.

During one freezing, bitter night in uniform, I imagined the terror of being lost in the Yukon, as in "To Build a Fire".

1988

FATAL DESIRE

Through my door and into the storm
Across mountainous drifts, a lonely form
Trudging onward past silence's lake
Footprints of oblivion in quiet's wake.

Into whiteness, solitude whispers sleep
Sleep not! A rendezvous to keep
Drowning, fragile flakes slowly kill
Courageous, determined naive will.

Slumber warmed a frigid breath
Vanished trail, vanished form - snow death
In the swirling pearl-gems grand
Peaceful serenity blankets the land.

After I played pool in the Golden Cue parlor in Queens, I remembered my youth and a champion from yesterday.

1980

James P. McMann

DOWNTOWN BILLIARDS, 1954

I remember skipping school to go downtown
To a place of mystery and envied renown
Up one flight of creaking stairs
Ten green-felted tables in this lair

Long windows, shades drawn to hide
A world of intrigue from the outside
Cues at attention in racks on walls
A phrase shimmering in mystique--"pool hall"

Runyonesque characters drift in this place
"Pete the Snake", "Old Man Spider", "Scarface"
Smell of powder, clicking of spheres
Combined intoxicant of safety and fear

Then all eyes surround Table One
Worshipping the man and the balls he'd run
"Fritz" circled, always gasping breath
Cruel emphysema was taking him to death

Roadman of wonder, his countless tales
Of conquest in Pooldom, how he was hailed!
Destroying all comers, deflating the best
Victory's arena, smoky, tiring, no rest

Eternity came for him in January cold
There were no shooters at his earthly hold
Just an aged pool shark in stillness lay
Downtown Billiards still opened that day.

*I knew two young
pool sharks in Queens
whose free will caused
their destruction.
1989*

James P. McMann

DEATH OF POOL SHARKS

Unlighted are the green felts of honor
Silent are the brightly colored balls
No rustling of human movement
Death stands alone in the billiard hall

"Fat Steve" was an oversized man
Who could pocket with all the best
Until that poison entered his arm
And swept him away to his final rest

"Fast Shooting Sammy" was a joy to see
Running through racks with effortless ease
Until hatred followed him home that day
Firing into his head after forcing him on his knees

Why did these pool sharks die so young?
What dark corner did they wrongfully turn?
What evil forces held them so close?
Why was it too late for them to learn?

For free will is a glorious gift
And it lets us make our permanent choice
To climb to sunlight or fall from grace
It all comes down to the inner voice

So Sammy and Steve will enter no more
To amaze all eyes with their skill
They being human with all of our faults
Who went to destruction with their free will

The hall will open, for tomorrow is another day
And memories are short when it comes to them
Talked about for moments that never last
New days, new month - soon new sharks -
    And they will be forgotten.

Unseen scars appear on the hearts of Police Officers when crimes against children are investigated. Written in police memo book about inner pain.

1987

James P. McMann

TIMES SQUARE COP

Observer of the river's light
Sees the illusions grinning bright
Masking all demons' hideous fright
Who lead the lost into eternal night

Uniformed human patrols Times Square
Knowing the ugly from the fair
Feeling all creatures beneath the glare
Paralyzing their desires with a stare

Tourists gape at Broadway's dream
Success with fame in flickering beams
Not hearing the agony within the gleam
Of tortured children's terrified screams

Slithering in the "White Way" mile
Devils who lure boys in fatherly style
Their words drip with lustful bile
Seducers of children, the pedophiles

Only the cop with silver shield
Valiantly forces the monsters to yield
All youngsters from their killing fields
Hoping someday that they be healed

Just one crime in Times Square roar
That hardens quickly sensitivity's core
Cynical bullets into cop's heart bore
Casualty of this street soldier's war.

> *Every   police
> precinct has a booking
> desk as you enter   the
> station house.   This was
> written while I was   on
> restricted duty, beholding
> the human parade.*
> *1989*

THE DESK

Before this wood stand the fallen
Some with defiant truth, others lying
Dressed in silk suits or smelly rags
With raving laughter or childish crying

Like a parade through Dante's gate
Killers with grins, rapists' shouts
Blood stained hands, destroyers of honor
Brilliant slayers and seducing louts

Viewing all this behind the desk
Men and women dressed in blue
Observers of the seamy human race
Protectors of society in what they do

They do not judge the passing scene
The sins are too numerous for them to sort
Their sentences are brief in this worldly life
Eternal verdicts are left to a higher court.

*An abandoned
lighthouse photo called me
to remember Melville's
brilliance in depicting pride,
revenge and death.
1987*

James P. McMann

WATCHING AHAB

This house of light saw them drown
Their captain to a whale was bound
Being rewarded for his pride
To his alter ego he was tied

All this the house has seen
Playing horribly in its beam
A mission of conquest ends in death
Waves of vengeance smother all breath

And today the cold light sees no more
But to poets is seen a door
Leading to fathomed chambers gray
Where bones of innocent and guilty lay

Gigantic ghostly creature looms
Colossal specter in sunken tomb
Rising mountain gleaming bright
Raging snowstorm, brilliantly white

And within its eternal noble race
A rubbery mask, Ahab's face
Gurgling words he only hears
"Melville, Melville, I curse you for my tears."

.

*"Scarface", Freddy
Franier, was a pool shark
unequaled, and in his face I
remembered loneliness.
1989*

James P. McMann

YESTERDAY'S ROADMAN

Ribbons of highway look all the same
Ending in parlors of different names
Waiting, all challengers for alluring fame
Call me "Scarface Freddy", Nineball's my game

Cheap motel, with its cut-out room
Smoky hall where anticipation looms
Victory sends a young shark to doom
I go back to loneliness of my tomb

Out on the road, another town near
One-night abode, empty cries I hear
Into hearts of pride, conquest drives fear
Shattering ego's reward, worshipping cheers

From city to city, with courage I roam
Enjoying destruction of braggarts who groan
Accused of playing with heart of stone
Only I know the misery, drifting alone.

Beneath the teeming anthill
called New York, steel
serpents race with humans
inside.

1986

James P. McMann

UNDERGROUND WORLD

Faces staring, not caring
Garbage strewn floors, broken sliding doors
Stressful, never on time
Monster on board, crime
Pushing, cursing, hating
Empty stations, waiting, waiting
Smelling, rotting lost souls
Bag people living like moles
Many disgusting sights to see
Moronic writing, graffiti
Unknown people to unknown places
Frozen, me-only faces.

"More tragic than being killed in the line of duty." Alone after the service, I wrote this in the church.

1987

James P. McMann

WEAKNESS IN US ALL

Attended a cop's funeral today
February was bitter, frozen, gray
Muffled drums, warpipes grand
Final salute from an Irish band

Blue coat columns - answers sought
Human frailty painfully taught
Ebony hearse carried him still
Stone cold church quickly filled

Eulogies spoken by grieving friends
Yet broken hearts will never mend
From reality's light no one hides
Our brother dead. . . . suicide

Remember him growing, handsome and fair
Shattered in one act of lonely despair
Comrades and family, who is to blame?
Signs of warning all could name

No one acted, really no one's fault
Decision of destruction, impossible to halt
Self-hate calling, no place to run
Drowning sorrow, escape! A gun!

Lowering the casket into the ground
Above the Taps, sobbing sounds
City protector from terror and strife
Another cop who took his life.

*Palaces   o f
glittering   illusions   o n
Broadway brought back
visions of movie houses
from yesterday.
1986*

James P. McMann

LAFAYETTE AND WASHINGTON

Three glowing palaces on a city block
Evening starships glittering late
Enticing two brothers aboard, inside
Scenes of my youth - 1948

Utica, Avon, Olympic
Brilliant vessels to make-believe lands
Where Robby and I would let swords clash
Comrades of Flynn in Robin Hood's band

Both of our parents were working each night
Boys left with no place to go
Escaped into theaters in order to find
Silver beam of illusion - picture show

Technicolor river swept us along
As a boy stalked the tiger to its lair
Valiant hero of Kipling's "Jungle Book"
Sabu, courageous youth so fair

Through black-white blazing gangster reels
Mesmerized lads glued to their seats
As Jimmy Cagney loses his world
Atop flaming gas tank in "White Heat"

All enchantment vanished when homeward bound
In tomorrow new wonderments hide
Counting long hours until that time
Away to the Stars, our rocket ride.

Poetry in Blue

*Written in remembrance
of my youth.
1979*

James P. McMann

REFLECTIONS

When I was a kid a thousand years ago
And the smell of Mom's cooking filled the air
And my father coming home tired and strong
Oh, if I could only go back and show I did care
You can't go back a thousand years
And race down the block and up the back stairs
And into a sanctuary that no longer exists
For yesterday is dead and, as with the dead,
No one cares.

*While driving
through Central Park one
frigid day in winter I looked
at the ice fingered trees
and thought of them with
sadness . . .*
1994

AUTUMN

Children desert their mother's arms
Forgetting her warm May charms
Sailing off in brilliant hues
Shades of purple, scarlet, golden blue

Floating down in silent swirls
Costumed ballerinas in final twirls
Each child falls at His command
Gently touched by creation's hand

Naked mothers stand frozen in death
Waiting in ice for returning breath
When children from their boughs appear
Cuddling green babies dry their tears.

Poetry in Blue

I wrote this after countless runs to these foul dungeons and the lost elderly who exist there.
1975

James P. McMann

OLD FOLKS HOME

Rooms of dreams, lost, forgotten
Lives that slowly melt away
Attended by stern, uncaring faces
Just waiting for death to come one day

And He arrives on silent wings
To call a name and touch a hand
Then sweetly lead a broken soul
To youth eternal in a glorious land

Those who hear not His voice
Just watch the departing of a friend
Hoping that they will leave fairly soon
Out of this life where they pretend

To exist in name only, for visiting family
Wanting the peace of the restful grave
Having trudged to the archway of time
Desiring only their souls to save

New bed sheets for the newly arrived
A small room, dreams of youth await
"Oh please Dear Lord, I beg of You
Do not let this death home be my fate!"

*A look at life
imitating life on stage.
1985*

James P. McMann

ILLUSIONS ON THE STAGE OF LIFE

In his plays, Williams subjected woman to disgrace
Wagner raised womanhood to noblest realms
For upon the stage, as in glorious life
Writers try to explain why women overwhelm

She can, in some men's eyes, be seductive, evil bred
Or valiant flaming warrior, forever radiantly pure
Performing before all eyes a written created world
Two images that for some, until death, will endure

So choose your lady with an observer's open mind
Not as the writer's moods, always black, always white
Take care to remember that only writers cast them so
For the less brilliant, they are whatever you see them in
        your sight.

Rethinking the murder of Caesar, and how centuries can change, but human nature remains the same.

1982

James P. McMann

BRUTUS' MIRROR

Accolades and laurels are never for long
With the fading day, so rusts the armor of praise
And the once givers of loudest applause
Will plot your downfall in envious ways

So beware of the flatterer's silver voice
As he exalts you and asks you to stand
For fanfares in honor of your achievements great
Then swiftly he rushes you with dagger in hand

Plunging so deeply as if to change all destiny
So fell Caesar, once cherished, divinely high
Murdered not by comrades, but blood drinking fools
Killing a regal legend; even eagles fall and die.

*On vacation I wrote
this after finding a broken
stone stairway of a forest
home.*

1980

STEPS GOING NOWHERE

I came upon stone steps one day
Deep within the woods, far from life
Broken and worn by yesterday's weight
Trodden by feet that knew joy and strife

Five stone steps climbing to nothing
An ancient ladder that carried all to light
The gleam of hospitality in someone's home
Taking the traveler into friendship bright

I rubbed the coarse face of broken slate
Feeling the tired climbers that once were there
Or sensing the racing feet of laughing children
Then seeing the reality that ages bare

Steps going nowhere in today's modern race
Left as a reminder to searchers like me
Telling of homes that all were now dust
Pure contemplation for my mind's eye to see.

Poetry in Blue

The Hudson River's
frozen face inspired a look
into ice dreams.
1987

James P. McMann

NOVEMBER VOICES
ALONG THE HUDSON

Bright short-lived days
Fading brilliant rainbow haze
River sings on, ice flows coming
Brisk air will soon be numbing

Trees sighing, their majesty falling
Drifting costumed leaves calling
Evergreens, emerald sentries on guard
The death of Winter they have barred

Moving silent water, shimmering glass
Squadrons of geese landing enmasse
It's a time for Nature to be bravely bold
Rearming her children against the approaching cold

Graying November, like Roman soldiers closing ranks
Protects herself in forests, along river banks
As a phalanx, shielded from frozen ice arrows
Leaving lonely man to face the onrushing, freezing
    perils.

*Marble sepulchers
in a cemetery reminded me
of unforgiveness and how
it becomes leprosy for
eternity.*
1987

REGRETS

The corpses of yesterday are in their tombs
Quiet and still, asleep in peace
Flee from wanting to awaken them
Let your regretting memory cease

From clamoring upon their sepulcher door
Life is for the living, not the departed
For they know the earthly hurts they've done
Forgive them and you'll be peace-hearted

Give mercy to them, with compassionate prayers
They will thank you in unexpected ways
By joining loved ones in reunion's tears
And you will thank God all your remaining days.

Poetry in Blue

We investigated
the death of a man whom
neighbors described as a
mean, wealthy miser. I
wrote this later.
1986

James P. McMann

AWAKENED FROM SLEEP

In a darkened catacomb he felt a door
From his moldering garments he fired a match
Serpentine hall twisted before his eyes
As the flickering revelation ended, a latch

Creaking open, the portal breathed a putrid smell
A sucking wind drew him in terror through
Twilight world of creatures yawned ahead
Above birds within human faces in millions flew

Half fish, half eagle picked him up in its claw
Brought its captive close to gilled beak
The monster sniffed his fading burial clothes
"No one wanted you at our door. Whom do you seek?"

"You have odor of luxury, a worldly life.
I will place you in the desert of your breed
Many of your plotters dwell there now
Furnace storms await in the Valley of Greed."

*Charlatans in
psychiatry and the strange
world of the mind.
1990*

PLANET UNKNOWN

Gilded palaces where victims speak
To charlatans, deceivers of the weak
In darkness they hopelessly try to find
Labyrinth of ebony, unexplored, the mind

Freud's name through history soars
Using controlled sleep to find a door
Only to realize there are numberless keys
Once opened, hundreds of portals to see

Explorers who venture to this sphere
Are lost in a twisted maze, never clear
No ship arrives in this unreal land
Divinely perplexing, molded by creation's hand

Jet-splashed mountains where genius flies
Onyx-drenched valleys hear madness cry
Planet beyond the beyond of reason's light
Featureless world, blinding logic's sight

Like a diamond with a child of earth
It comes glowing, untrampled at birth
Glittering treasure chest of given gold
Untouchable, unattainable, in its secret hold

Human probes will never reach this star
Within ourselves, yet illusively far
Only at death will mortal chains break
Cleansing all boundaries in eternity's lake.

Written after I helped investigate a suicide from the Willis Avenue Bridge in the Bronx. 1985

THE GATE KEEPER

The stranger stopped and quietly asked
"Excuse me Sir, but I have lost my way.
I awoke and found myself in this strange place
And the dark frightens me, so help me, I pray."

The keeper smiled a haunting, toothless grin
"Stranger, the path you seek is through my gate
And once you pass alone with my aid
You will be welcomed into our city of hate"

"City of hate? My God, what do you mean?"
The stranger's mind raced back before his dark sleep
And terror, sheer terror lighted his thoughts
Illuminating the dark waters into which he did leap

Then the great gray bridge came into view
And he saw himself gazing downward, pondering his fate
His free will allowed his eternally foolish choice
So the gate creaked open, for this stranger it was too late

The gate keeper never sleeps at his damning post
He has met millions of strangers with tales to tell
All lost in his company, all seeking his help
For his name is cruelty and his gate leads to Hell.

*After finishing a 6
PM to 2 AM tour, I took the
train at 42nd and 8th
Avenue downtown. The
subway station was a maze
of forgotten misery. Written
aboard the "E" train.
1988*

James P. McMann

SUBWAY AFTER MIDNIGHT

Venture down beneath the street
To the confines of roaring, dirty trains
Into the foul breathing air of human waste
Observing the frightened, lonely ragged, insane

For in this metropolis of power-drenched wealth
Exists a tortured army of living despair
Moving like the undead from Stoker's book
Fearing the sunlight, making this hopelessness' lair

Screamers and babblers, ragers untold
Possibly once happy people in life's plan
Until incurable diseases invaded their minds
Dooming them to darkness in this once bright land

Compassion is the divinely given flower of the soul
But these forlorn castoffs will never this treasure breathe
In this self-centered creation that cares not for living
Until through Death's merciful door, they leave.

*After I retired, I
went back to the Midtown
North Precinct and felt the
true, crushing pain of the
outsider.*
1990

James P. McMann

LONGING

Through the entrance I slowly go
Into a chaos only cops know
Shields of bravery, warriors wear
One New York precinct, Times Square

All is familiar but can never be the same
A locker stands uneasy with another's name
Denying your career's sun has set
Memories shattered by reality, regret

"Oh steel hands of time, you cruelly flew
From comradeship of soldiers, valiant blue"
Retired cop departs this never-ending war
Voice of truth: "You don't belong anymore."

I was stationed at St. Patrick's Cathedral, and would have been killed there, were it not for the grace of God. Written while recovering in Bellevue Hospital.
1988

ST. PATRICK'S

Cathedral mighty, God's sanctuary of peace
Doorway to redemption, majesty and prayer
Beckoning all travelers to meditate and pause
Adoration of our Maker for all to share

Outside the edifice the roaring city streams
Inside its candles sing, burning songs of hope
Outside the world dances without worry or care
Inside its glories bless people with courage to cope

No terrors or horrors had crossed its door
Till the night when murder came creeping in
Taking hold of a tortured wanderer of the streets
The murderer was controlled by the creator of Sin

Then, in that chaotic moment of madness possessed
John Winter, an usher, was brutally slain
Committing the crime within the confines of grace
Acted out not by man, but by the Deceiver of Cain

The Cathedral calls people from every lands
Brings all men healing, make them spiritually well
Within its confines prevails the knowledge
That nothing can harm it, not even the Gates of Hell.

Down the street or around the corner from the station house there is a place where the terrors of the job can be briefly washed away.
1989

COPS' BAR

Precinct bar, "The Silver Shield",
Stationhouse pub down the street
Raw nerves, momentarily healed
American soldiers, weary, meet

Over smoky bourbon and vile gin
Horror tales through courage wend
United in war they cannot win
Cops talking to cops, their only friends

This is a world civilians can't know
Closed society, a moment in time
Laughter and terror, in secret, flow
Around-the-clock destroyers of crime

Some depart, homeward bound
Army leaving, it's getting late
Lonely stay for one last round
Tomorrow's terrors silently wait.

Terror can come to cops at any hour. The encounter that follows happened as most people were rising for work.
1984

THE PASSENGER

Called to the Hudson at dawn
Black coffee was conquering sleep
Curious to the river were drawn
A car pushed into the deep

Police divers, cable in hand
Winched from the depths with a reel
Sunken Caddy back to the land
Bloated corpse cuffed to the wheel

Vehicle swayed above stone pier
Gray water poured from this crypt
Tough cops observe without fear
Terror! Bulging eyes, purple lips

Five thousand bucks, chain of gold
To a loan shark he had lied
Possessions intact from his watery hold
Something else: An eel from his insides

Thought about the killers, hearing him sob
Shackling their prey, securing tight
Murder contract ordered by the mob
Drowning screams as he sank from sight

Gawkers departing this act of Cain
Only the morbid need to stay
Cops' dry humor eases the pain
Late tour ending, another day.

Poetry in Blue

James P. McMann

FIRE SOLDIERS

Fire soldiers, Forty-Eight and Eighth
Respond to continual calls
Raging orange infernos
Collapsing tenement walls

Ladders go up to terrified faces
Melting flames horribly creep
Choices made in suicide scream
Into eternity all leap

Panicked humans swiftly plunge
Fallen angels and sidewalk meet
Exploding balloons of scarlet paint
Flight of death in escaping heat

Meals never finished at Forty-Eighth and Eighth
Foghorn bellows as red doors rise
Trucks roar out, army on board
Ahead, hellish enemy lies.

I remember a wake
that my mother and I
attended. I was only nine,
and terrified. My mom softly
laughed.
1980

THE WAKE OF FRANKIE O'SHEA

Murphy's funeral home was open all night
Just candles dancing in eerie light
The sorrowful filed slowly on by
With silence briefly broken by sighs

On past the bier they glancing, marched
At the sleeper, all powdered and starched
Gleaming with carefully brushed paint
Only one young woman did faint

The slumberer's mother Kate and sister Claire
Were the only ones for the nightly prayers
All the rest were in an adjoining room
Around them the aroma of Irish whiskey loomed

No tears for the dreamer from this thirsty crew
Just gossip from their wagging tongues flew
Tales of the deceased in bolder times
Stories of his loves, his faith, his crimes

The whiskey room door burst open
Out staggered six burly men
Who swaying, stumbled up to his bier
Then lifted him out with a slurred cheer

Holding him high in a strange act of flight
Mother Kate, sister Claire, fainted at the sight
Marched around the room with him overhead
Just the intoxicated living with the sober dead

Placed back down by his rescuing kin
Across his face there spread such a grin
Happy that his cronies gave him a ride
The bottle of Irish tucked by his side

So they buried him in the February cold
Six knowing he would be warm in his earthly hold
For, within an hour no mourners could be found
Just the graveyard silence, except for gurgling sounds.

James P. McMann

James P. McMann performs excellent dramatic readings of his poetry. If your organization would like Jim to appear at your store, school, theater or meeting, please contact the Events Coordinator at:

Good Times Publishing Company
PO Box 4545
Utica, NY 13504

Poetry in Blue